# I love Mom

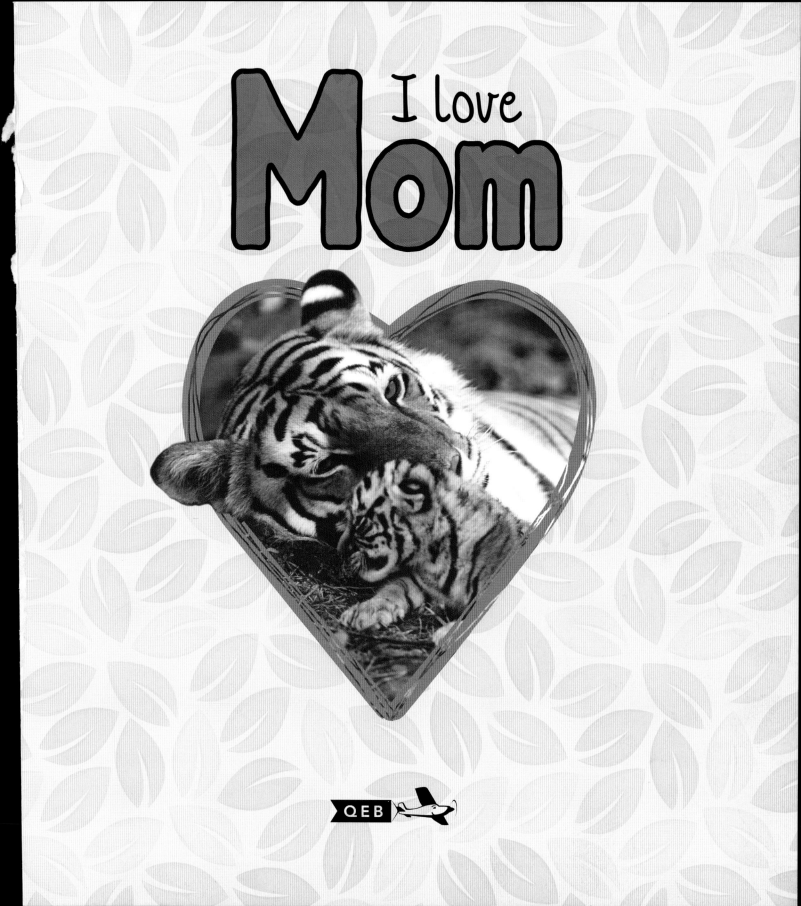

QEB

A Mom's love for her child is **unconditional**, even in the animal kingdom.

We all need our **Moms** to protect, nurture, and look after us.

Baby animals love their **Moms** and learn from them every day, just like us.

# I'm so glad I look like you, Mom, because your face is beautiful.

Koalas are marsupials, which means a mother keeps her baby in a special pouch. When a koala baby is too big for the pouch, it clings onto its mother's back while she clambers through eucalyptus trees.

# I'm just going to stretch my legs and rest my chin on your head. You don't mind, do you, Mom?

Cheetah cubs use their mother for hunting practice by jumping on her and grabbing hold of her neck or head. They are learning the moves that will help them survive when they are older and must find their own food.

# Oh no, it's all gone dark. Where is everyone?

Piping plovers are great parents. They let their chicks huddle underneath them to keep warm. They even pretend to be injured so other animals attack them, not their babies.

# Your smile lights up my world.

A dolphin calf can swim as soon as it is born. It gets an easy ride by staying next to its mother. As she moves through the water the calf is pulled along, too. Dolphins "talk" to each other with clicks and whistles.

I know you want the best for me, Mom. Wherever you lead, I will follow.

Mother elephants and their babies have a very close, loving bond. Female calves often stay with their mothers all their lives, and grandmothers help raise the next generation of youngsters.

# We're playing hide and seek. Don't tell Mom where I'm hiding!

A baby kangaroo is called a joey. The joey climbs into its mother's pouch as soon as it has been born, and is no bigger than a jelly bean. A pouch is a safe place to drink Mom's milk and grow bigger.

# Sometimes the world looks big and scary, but I feel safe when I'm close to my Mom.

The world is a scary place for a gazelle because lions and hyenas are on the lookout for animals to hunt. Mothers force their newborn babies onto their feet so they will be ready to run if there is any sign of danger.

# My Mom's always there for me, even when I need a little nudge...

Hippos are huge, heavy animals that spend most of the day wallowing in cool water. They have massive teeth—up to 20 inches long—and can deliver a deadly bite to anyone who comes too close to their calves.

# You always offer me a shoulder to cry on when I'm feeling sad.

Lemurs only live on the island of Madagascar. Most lemur mothers carry their babies everywhere they go until they are at least four months old. They feed them, clean them, and teach them how to find food.

# LOOK at me, Mom! LOOK at what I can do!

Baby orangutans cling to their mothers until they are about two years old, but they are learning from her all of the time. They like to grab hold of branches and practice swinging, or gripping with their fingerlike toes—but they always keep Mom close by!

# I promise
to have a
bath, Mom...
right after
you have had
yours.

Gray wolves live in family groups
called packs. Only the top male and
female in a pack have cubs, but all
the wolves work together to protect
the family and hunt for food. Cubs
are born blind, deaf, and helpless.

# I love you SO much. I just want to cuddle with you forever!

Polar bears live in one of the world's coldest places. They have incredibly thick fur so they can cope with icy wind, and they can even swim in chilly Arctic waters. Their white color helps to camouflage them in the snow.

# My Mom supports me in everything I do. She is my rock.

Mother walruses are huge, but male walruses grow twice as big—up to 12 feet long! Walrus pups climb onto their mother's back so they can watch the world from a safe place without getting squashed by clumsy males!

# Mom says it's time for bed. Sweet dreams!

Sloths live in rain forest trees. They move so slowly that plants can grow in their fur, giving it a greenish tinge. They sleep while hanging upside down, and only clamber down to the ground once a week, when it is time to poop!

# Here are three ways to show Mom you love her.

Give her a big hug.

♥

Draw her a beautiful picture.

♥

Ask her about her day.

## Can you think of any more?

Copyright © QEB Publishing, Inc. 2014

First published in the United States by
QEB Publishing, Inc.
6 Orchard
Lake Forest, CA 92630

ISBN 978 1 60992 919 0

Manufactured in Guandong, China
Lot #:
2 4 6 8 10 9 7 5 3
12/15

Editor: Tasha Percy
Editorial Assistant: Joanna McInerney
Editorial Director: Victoria Garrard
Designer: Natalie Godwin
Art Director: Laura Roberts-Jensen
Publisher: Zeta Jones

Photo credits
(t=top, b=bottom, l=left, r=right, c=center, fc=front cover)
1c: Getty Images: Tom Brakefield, 2l: Shutterstock: Vic and Julie Pigula, 3r: Shutterstock:
Background, 4l: istockphoto.com: Background, 5r: Getty Images: Bobby-Jo Clow, 6l:
Getty Images: Winifried Wisniewski, 7r: Shutterstock: Background, 8l: Shutterstock:
Background, 9r: istockphoto.com: © Ken Canning, 10l: Getty Images: Eco/UIG, 11r:
istockphoto.com: Background, 12l: Shutterstock: Background, 13r: Getty Images: Gallo
Images-Michael Poliza, 14l: Getty Images: Auscape/UIG, 15r: Shutterstock: Background,
16l: istockphoto.com: Background, 17r Getty Images: Gallo Images - Heinrich van den
Berg, 18l: Corbis: Ken Bohn, 19r: istockphoto.com: Background, 20l; Shutterstock:
Background, 21r: Getty Images: Cyril Ruoso/ Minden Pictures, 22l: FLPA: Suzi
Eszterhas, 23r: Shutterstock: Background, 24l: Shutterstock: Background, 25r: Getty
Images: Ronald Wittek, 26l: © Christine V. Haines, 27r: Shutterstock: Background, 28l:
istockphoto.com: Background, 29r: Getty Images: Paul Nicklen, 30l: NaturePL: Roland
Seitre 31r: istockphoto.com: Background, 32c: Shutterstock: Background